YOUR FIRST
20 DEALS

TONY SOWTER
Foreword by BOBBY WOLFF

HOW TO PLAY BRIDGE

NTC Publishing Group
NTC/Contemporary Publishing Group

Library of Congress Cataloging-in-Publication Data is on file at the United States Library of Congress

Published by NTC Publishing Group
An imprint of NTC/Contemporary Publishing Group
Copyright © 2000 Tony Sowter
4255 West Touhy Avenue, Lincolnwood (Chicago)
Illinois 60646- 1975 U.S.A.

Printed in Singapore
International Standard Book Number:
0-8442-2229-1

contents

foreword by Bobby Wolff   4

introduction   6

your first rubber:
deals 1-4   7

your second rubber:
deals 5-10   27

ten more deals:
deals 11-20   52

foreword

Bridge is a game enjoyed by many millions of players all over the world.

In these days of rising commercial pressures, increasing leisure and greater longevity, bridge has the potential to break down social and ethnic barriers and to keep the wheels of the brain turning in both the old and the young. Apart from that, bridge at whatever level is a very inexpensive game; all you need to play is a flat surface that the four players can sit round with a pack of cards and, of course, an understanding as to how to play the game.

It is for these reasons that I am particularly pleased to welcome the 'How to Play Bridge' series which has been specially designed to make the game easy to follow for beginners, no matter what their age. I believe that you will find the whole series well presented and particularly easy to read.

It is a curious fact, that over the years many of the great bridge authors have been British. Names like Victor Mollo, Hugh Kelsey, Skid Simon and Terence Reese still figure prominently in the USA lists of the greatest selling bridge books, so the fact that this series of books has been generated in Great Britain comes as no real surprize. I happen to know that all the authors have played bridge at International level so, in general terms, they should

know what they are talking about. Furthermore, all
of the books are based on the methods that are
played all over the United States today. So, once
you have learned, you should have little difficulty
in getting a game whenever you want to.

I believe that after studying the 'How to Play Bridge'
series you will not only be off to a good start, you
will be totally enthralled by this great game.

Bobby Wolff
Dallas, Texas
March 1997

introduction

Welcome to the greatest game of them all.

This book divides into three parts. In Your First
Rubber, you are shown all four hands right from
the start of every deal. The idea is that you use
these four deals to give yourself a good idea as to
how the mechanics of the game work. Take out a
pack of cards and lay them out as shown in the
hand diagram and then follow both the bidding
and the play through.

The next six deals comprise, Your Second Rubber.
In many ways, from a technical point of view these
hands are easier than the first four deals however
you can only see the North and South hands to
start with, so planning the play might just be that
little bit harder. Once again, don't hesitate to use a
pack of cards to trace through all the action.

The same format is maintained for Ten More Deals
but this section introduces some slightly more
advanced concepts in both bidding and play.

Good luck.

deal 1

A rubber is a set of deals which comes to an end when one of the partnerships has made two games. As it happens, *Your First Rubber* comprises the first four deals of this book. Unlike real life, you can actually see the location of all 52 cards in the pack. So, use a pack of cards to try and follow the play.

Here is the first deal:

Dealer South.
Neither side vulnerable (No score)

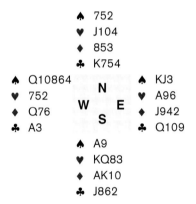

```
              ♠  752
              ♥  J104
              ♦  853
              ♣  K754
   ♠ Q10864        N      ♠ KJ3
   ♥ 752                  ♥ A96
   ♦ Q76      W     E     ♦ J942
   ♣ A3           S       ♣ Q109
              ♠  A9
              ♥  KQ83
              ♦  AK10
              ♣  J862
```

South's hand is much better than average. For the purpose of evaluating just how strong the hand is, adopt the standard high card point system which values an ace as four points, a king as three, a queen as two and a jack as one. As there are four of

each, the total number of points in the pack is 40, so an average hand will include 10 high card points.
In this example, South has four points in spades, five in hearts, seven in diamonds and one in clubs – a total of 17 points, which is a lot better than average and rather more than the minimum to open the bidding which is normally about 13 points.

The other important feature about this South hand is that it is balanced. In general hands of a 4-3-3-3, 4-4-3-2 and 5-3-3-2 distribution are regarded as balanced. They are only three out of a possible 39 distribution types, but they account for nearly half of all possible hands.

High card point count

A = 4
K = 3
Q = 2
J = 1

In most bridge bidding systems an opening bid of 1NT shows a balanced hand within a fairly narrow range of points. You are going to use a strong no trump opening with the opening bid of 1NT showing between 16 and 18 high card points.

Consequently, on this deal, South should open the bidding with a bid of 1NT.

The bidding moves on clockwise (starting with the dealer) round the table, so it is West's turn to bid next.

How many points does West have?

In fact, West has eight points, two in spades, two in diamonds and four in clubs. Eight points is less than average so West has no real interest in suggesting that his side should play the hand. Therefore, West should pass.

It is North's turn next. North has four points. One in hearts and three in clubs. He might have been sad when he picked up such a weak hand but he should have cheered up when he heard South open 1NT. North knows that his side has between 20 and 22 points – hopefully enough to make seven tricks. However, North should have no expectation of making more, so North should pass.

Finally, the spotlight turns on East.

How many high card points does East have?

East has 11 high card points, four in spades, four in hearts, one in diamonds and two in clubs.

What should East bid?

While East's hand is slightly better than average he also knows that South has between 16 and 18 high card points. If South has, say 17, that only leaves 12 between West and North. If those points were evenly divided then West, East's partner, would only have six points and East/West will be heavily outgunned. With no long suit of his own, it would be very dangerous for East to bid, therefore East should pass.

So, the bidding looks like this:

South	West	North	East
1NT	Pass	Pass	Pass

the play

Many players all over the world follow the maxim of leading '4th best' of their longest and strongest suit against no trumps, so in this case West leads the ♠6.

The North hand goes down on the table as dummy. The North player takes no further part in this deal, as South, declarer, will choose which cards to play from dummy as well as which cards to play from his own hand. However, before playing a card from dummy, declarer should consider his line of play.

How many top winners does South have?

He can only count three top winners – the ace of spades and the ace and king of diamonds. So to make seven tricks he needs to find four more.

Where can these come from?

If declarer knocks out the ace of hearts, that will give him three heart tricks taking his total to six and the remaining trick will have to come from clubs.

Let's play the hand. On the ♠6 lead, declarer plays the ♠2 from dummy, and East should play his highest spade, the ♠K. Following his plan, declarer wins the ♠A and plays the ♥3 to the ♥2, ♥10 and ♥A. East now plays the ♠J. West overtakes with his ♠Q (in case East only had two spades) and continues by cashing the ♠10, ♠8 and then the ♠4. Declarer can safely discard one diamond and one club from

the dummy and from his own hand, so he
throws the ♦10 and two small clubs.
West then plays a diamond to East's
♦9 and South's ♦K.

   Declarer can safely cash his hearts
now, playing the ♥8 to dummy's ♥J
and a heart back to his queen. When
declarer plays the ♥K, West discards the
♣3, dummy the ♣5 and East the ♣9.

The actual position now looks like this:

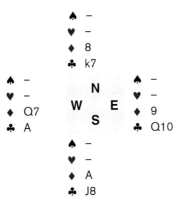

```
                ♠  –
                ♥  –
                ♦  8
                ♣  k7
     ♠  –                      ♠  –
     ♥  –           N          ♥  –
     ♦  Q7       W     E       ♦  9
     ♣  A           S          ♣  Q10
                ♠  –
                ♥  –
                ♦  A
                ♣  J8
```

Declarer has already made five tricks and the ♦A
is an obvious sixth. However, if South cashes his
♦A now, he will go down, for West will make the
last two tricks with the ♣A and the ♦Q. So, South
must play a club now. It is true to say that, if East
had both the ♣A and the ♣Q South would go
down but in that case he could never have made
the seven tricks required to fulfil his contract.

By playing a club now, South will succeed as the cards lie. West wins his ♣A and must play a diamond. Declarer wins the last two tricks with the ♦A and the ♣K.

South has made 1NT exactly and scores 40 points below the line – meaning that these 40 points will count towards making the 100 points needed to make a game. The deal passes clockwise after every hand, so West will be the dealer for our second hand.

points to remember

High Card Points (HCP) are an aid to measuring the strength of your hand. Count four for an ace, three for a king, two for a queen and just one for a jack.

If a hand is described as balanced, it has a flat distribution. Hands with a 4-3-3-3, 4-4-3-2 or 5-3-3-2 distribution are normally described as balanced.

1NT making seven tricks scores 40 points

An opening bid of 1NT shows a balanced hand in the range of 16-18 High Card Points.

Playing in no trumps, declarer should always start by counting his top winners and then working out how many extra tricks are needed to make his contract.

deal 2

Dealer West.
Neither side vulnerable. North/South +40

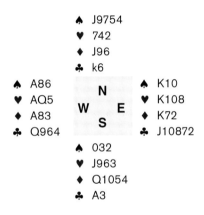

```
              ♠ J9754
              ♥ 742
              ♦ J96
              ♣ k6
   ♠ A86          N        ♠ K10
   ♥ AQ5                   ♥ K108
   ♦ A83      W     E      ♦ K72
   ♣ Q964         S        ♣ J10872
              ♠ 032
              ♥ J963
              ♦ Q1054
              ♣ A3
```

This time it is West to open the bidding.

How many points has West got?

Yes, West has 16 points – four in spades, six in
hearts, four in diamonds and two in clubs.

What should West bid?

Just like South in our first hand, West has a
balanced hand in the 16-18 point range, so West
should open 1NT. With only five points North will
pass and it becomes East's turn.

How many points does East have?

East has 10 points – three in spades, three in hearts, three in diamonds and one in clubs.

As a result, East should know that the combined East/West hands have between 26 and 28 points. Most of the time, 26 points should be enough to make game in no trumps, that is nine tricks.

So what should East bid?

East should bid what he thinks he can make, 3NT. Everyone passes, so the bidding has been:

South	West	North	East
–	1NT	Pass	3NT
Pass	Pass	Pass	

the play

What should North lead?

North should lead the ♠5, 4th best of his longest and strongest suit. While North's spades are not very strong this suit is still North/South's best chance of setting up tricks, especially from North's point of view.

The East hand comes down as dummy, and after considering his line of play, declarer, West, plays the ♠10 from dummy. South covers the ♠10 with the queen and declarer plays the ♠6. South returns the ♠3 to the ♠8, ♠ 4 and the ♠K. Declarer then plays the ♣2 from the dummy.

What should South play now?

South should play the ♣A. Perhaps the best way of explaining this is to look and see what happens if South plays a low club. West plays the ♣Q and North is forced to take the ♣K. North plays another spade, dummy discards a diamond while declarer wins the ♠A. Now West plays another club, South wins and having no more spades he must lead a red suit, so West makes two spades, three hearts, two diamonds and three clubs – a total of 10 tricks.

Now, contrast this with what happens if South plays the ♣A on the first round of the suit. South wins the trick with the ♣A and plays his last spade. West takes his ace and plays another club, but North wins this trick and now has two spade winners to cash to beat the contract by one trick.

North/South score 50 points for defeating West's contract by one trick. However, the score of +50 does not count towards North/South's target of 100 points to make game – it is purely a bonus score.

Note that, while South had to defend well to beat 3NT, it was all perfectly logical. When North was able to play the ♠4 on the second round, South 'knew' that North had started with five spades – after all, if the ♠5 was fourth best, the four must have been fifth best. Also, South knew that he had nine points himself and he could see 10 points in the dummy. As

West had announced a holding of 16-18 points, this left a maximum of five points for North (40-9-10-16 = 5). So, North could not possibly have more than one entry card outside spades.

In these circumstances, it was of paramount importance for South to grab the lead as quickly as possible in order to return his partner's suit and hope that North would get the lead later to cash his spade winners.

Now, as West failed to make his 3NT contract, you might be inclined to think that East bid too much when he jumped to 3NT. Far from it. Bridge is a game of probabilities and a game of mistakes. The truth of the matter is that West was unlucky, he would have made his contract:

(a) If the defense led any suit other than spades.

(b) If the spade suit had been divided evenly with four cards in both the North and South hands rather than 5 cards in North and only 3 cards in South.

(c) If South had both the ♣A and the ♣K.

(d) If North had 6 spades unless he also had both top club honours.

(e) If South hadn't been quite so awake in defense – and to be fair, it is much harder when you can't see all four hands.

points to remember

If you know that your side has enough points to make a game, make sure that you reach a game contract. If your partner opens 1NT and you have nine or more points then you should definitely be in a game contract.

Leading against no trumps, always try and lead your side's longest suit. Without any bidding from partner to guide you, lead fourth best of your longest and strongest suit.

Unless you have a good alternative, try and return partner's suit. Look for opportunities to win a trick at an early stage so that you can help establish partner's suit before declarer knocks out partner's entry cards.

deal 3

Dealer North.

Neither side vulnerable. North/South + 40

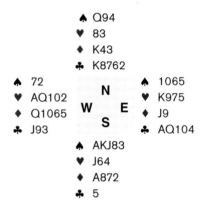

```
                    ♠ Q94
                    ♥ 83
                    ♦ K43
                    ♣ K8762
        ♠ 72                      ♠ 1065
        ♥ AQ102      N            ♥ K975
        ♦ Q1065    W   E          ♦ J9
        ♣ J93        S            ♣ AQ104
                    ♠ AKJ83
                    ♥ J64
                    ♦ A872
                    ♣ 5
```

As dealer, North has first shot at opening the bidding.

What should North bid?

North should pass as he only has eight points and you need 13 points to open the bidding.

As East only has 10 points he passes as well, so then it is South's turn to bid.

What should South bid?

South should open 1♠. South has 13 high card points but, when opening the bidding with a suit bid, opener can add on extra points for good distribution.

One point for each card more than four in any suit. So, as South has five spades, his hand is worth 14 points, more than enough to open the bidding.

In our system, openings of 1 ♥ and 1 ♠ show at least five cards in the suit bid. So, 1 ♠ is the obvious choice of opening.

West passes, so then it is North's turn to bid. Admittedly eight points is nothing to write home about, but the good news is that South has shown opening bid values with at least five spades. In support of spades, the North hand can be up-valued by one point for the doubleton heart. North should raise to 2 ♠, showing at least three spades and 6-10 points (high card and support points).

East passes. Now, what should South do?

While South has a reasonable hand, there is no point in getting higher than he needs to make game. Yes, if South makes 2 ♠, North/South will only score 60 points below the line, but as they already have 40 points from the first hand, 60 points more is all they need to make game. (Game = 100 or more points below the line.) So, South should pass.

West also passes, so, 2 ♠ becomes the contract.

The bidding has been:

West	North	East	South
–	Pass	Pass	1 ♠
Pass	2 ♠	Pass	Pass
Pass			

Support points:
Add 1 for a doubleton
Add 2 for a singleton
Add 3 for a void

the play

West leads the ♠7 and the North hand comes down as dummy, leaving South to try and make eight tricks with spades as trumps.

How many top winners does South have?

South has a total of seven winners. Five spade tricks and the two top diamonds. To make his contract, South only needs one more trick which might come from a number of places.

First, the diamonds might break evenly, with three cards in both the East and West hands but, as you can see, they don't. Then, club ace might be in the West hand in which case leading the ♣5 towards the king would establish a club trick. But, as you can see, East has the ♣A. There might be a better way. South is playing in a trump contract, so if he could score just one ruff in dummy that would yield the eighth trick. We could try and ruff (i.e. trump) a heart. If West hadn't led a trump, this would be easy – all we would have to do would be to surrender two hearts and then ruff the third one. But here that plan should fail.

Why?

The defense can prevent South from ruffing a heart in the dummy. West will win the first heart and play a second spade, then East will win the next heart and play his last spade. All this means that dummy will no longer have a trump left to ruff a heart with.

That doesn't seem to leave an obvious option – or does it? South should play the ♦K, the ♦A and another diamond. If diamonds break 3-3, he already has eight tricks – but if diamonds are 4-2 South will be able to trump his last diamond with the ♠Q.

Note that, in tougher circles, East/West might have competed to 3♥, a contract that would have have made as the ♣K is in the North hand. However, as it is, South played 2♠ very carefully to make eight tricks and score 60 points. With the 40 points on the first hand North/South have now made the first game, so, on the next deal, they will be vulnerable.

points to remember

An opening bid at the one level, in either major suit, shows 13 or more points and at least five cards in the suit bid.

Opener can add on extra points for good distribution. One point for each card more than four in any suit. So, add two points on for any hand with a six-card suit or a hand with two five-card suits.

A simple raise of one of a major to two of the major shows at least three trumps and 6-10 points (high card and support points).

After counting your top tricks and establishing how many extra tricks you need, consider whether you can make some of the extra tricks by ruffing in dummy.

deal 4

Dealer East. North/South vulnerable

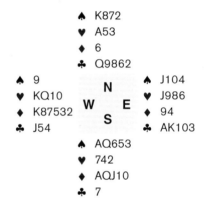

```
                    ♠ K872
                    ♥ A53
                    ♦ 6
                    ♣ Q9862
    ♠ 9                          ♠ J104
    ♥ KQ10        N              ♥ J986
    ♦ K87532   W     E           ♦ 94
    ♣ J54         S              ♣ AK103
                    ♠ AQ653
                    ♥ 742
                    ♦ AQJ10
                    ♣ 7
```

With only nine high card points, East passes as dealer.

What should South bid?

Just like last time, South should open 1♠. South has 13 high card points and five spades.

West passes. Now what should North bid?

Clearly this hand is much stronger than the last one where North simply raised 1♠ to 2♠. While North has only got nine high card points, the fourth trump plus the singleton diamond combine to produce a lot of ruffing potential. Indeed you would

fullness of time he will be able to ruff a heart in the dummy – also making 10 tricks. In particular, the heart discard from dummy stops the defense taking more that one heart and one club after winning the ♦K.

Making 4♠ scores +120, a second game and enough to win the rubber for North/South.

Here is the full score-sheet.

We North/South	They East/West
700 50	
40 60	
120	

North/South receive a bonus of 700 points for winning the rubber two games to nil. The total score adding up to North/South + 970.

points to remember

To raise a one of a major opening to three, you need 11 or 12 points (including support points) and at least three trumps.

If the responder raises a one of a major opening to three, opener should pass with a minimum opening bid but press on to game with any extra strength.

Always consider whether you can afford to draw trumps. In this example, you only need one trump left in dummy to do the necessary ruffing so you could remove any chance of the opponents scoring a trump trick by drawing trumps in three rounds before taking any ruffs in the dummy.

◆

So far, you have had the unrealistic advantage of seeing all four hands while you are playing. In the next section you will only see two of the hands until the play is finished. That makes the play correspondingly harder but, if you have followed the logic of the play on these first four deals, you should find the winning play on the next few deals.

deal 5

For the first rubber, you could see all four hands all
the time. Hopefully, this gave you a feel for both
the bidding and the play of the cards. Now the
time has come for you to see just the North
and South hands. You will be still be asked
what you would bid on both hands but
you will not see the opposition's
hands until later.

Dealer South.
Neither side vulnerable

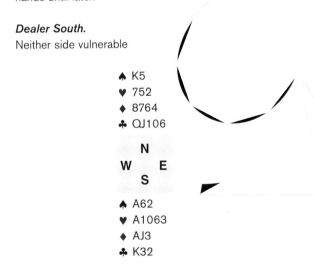

```
        ♠ K5
        ♥ 752
        ♦ 8764
        ♣ QJ106
           N
       W       E
           S
        ♠ A62
        ♥ A1063
        ♦ AJ3
        ♣ K32
```

What should South open?

South has a balanced hand with four points in
spades, four in hearts, five in diamonds and three
in clubs, a total of 16; enough to open 1NT.

West passes, what should North bid?

With only six points, North knows that the most points North/South can have between them is 24, not enough for game, so North should pass.

East also passes, so the final contract is 1NT, the full auction being:

South	West	North	East
1NT	Pass	Pass	Pass

the play

West leads the ♠Q, and the North hand is put down on the table as dummy, leaving South to try and make at least seven tricks.

What card should declarer play from dummy?

Take care. Declarer should not play a card from dummy before making a plan. Start with:

How many top tricks are there?

There are two tricks in spades, one in hearts and one in diamonds, a total of four, leaving South three tricks short of the target of seven.

Where will the other three tricks come from?

Obviously clubs. The suit is solid apart from the

fact that the ace is missing. Knocking out the ace should establish three extra tricks. It looks to be plain sailing, but South still needs to be careful as there are two separate traps to fall into.

For example, see what happens if South wins the ♠A, plays a low club to the queen and then the jack of clubs. If an opponent wins this round of the suit and play another spade, South will take the king, play a club to the king and then find that he can no longer get back to the dummy to cash the ♣10.

To avoid this trap South must be careful to play the ♣K on either the first or second round of the suit.

The second trap is a good illustration of why declarer should stop and make a plan before playing from the dummy at trick one. Suppose South wins the first trick with the ♠K. Then South carefully plays the ♣6 from the dummy to the king which holds the trick. Next he plays a small club back to the ten which also holds the trick. The queen of clubs follows and this time East wins the trick and plays another spade.

South wins with the ace but now there is no longer an entry back to the dummy to cash the remaining ♣J. One down once again.

Now, what card should declarer play from the dummy at trick one?

Yes, declarer must play the ♠5 and win the trick with the ace, so that he has a re-entry to the dummy after setting up the clubs.

The full deal:

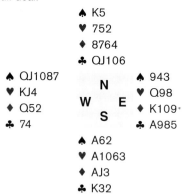

```
                 ♠ K5
                 ♥ 752
                 ♦ 8764
                 ♣ QJ106
  ♠ QJ1087           N      ♠ 943
  ♥ KJ4                     ♥ Q98
  ♦ Q52        W       E    ♦ K109
  ♣ 74               S      ♣ A985
                 ♠ A62
                 ♥ A1063
                 ♦ AJ3
                 ♣ K32
```

Provided South won the first spade with the ace,
and then knocked out the ♣A, remembering to
play the king on the first or second round, he
scored +40 below the line. Otherwise, South got
off to a poor start and East/West scored 50 bonus
points.

points to remember

Facing a 1NT opening showing 16-18 points, pass
if your hand is balanced with less than seven
points.

   In establishing even a solid looking suit such as
the club suit on this deal you must remember to
'unblock' the high honours from the short hand.
Here it was necessary to play the ♣K early.
It is no good establishing tricks in the dummy if
you have no entry left to get back to cash them.

deal 6

Dealer West

Neither side vulnerable. North/South +40

```
         ♠ J10976
         ♥ Q842
         ♦ 75
         ♣ Q4
              N
         W        E
              S
         ♠ K43
         ♥ J73
         ♦ A103
         ♣ J976
```

West opens 1NT. What should North bid?

With only five high card points, North should pass.

East raises to 3NT. What should South bid?

With no long suit and less than an average hand it
would be suicide to bid anything. South should
pass and hope to beat 3NT. Both West and North
pass, so the full bidding is:

South	West	North	East
–	1NT	Pass	3NT
Pass	Pass	Pass	

the play

North leads the jack of spades and dummy materialises with:

♠ A2
♥ 1096
♦ KQ942
♣ 1083

Declarer plays the two of spades from the dummy. What card do should South play?

South should win the trick with the king, of spades, declarer playing the five.

What should South play next?

North's lead of the ♠J will be the top card of a sequence, so, while South knows that declarer has the queen, North should hold the ten and possibly the nine as well. If North has led his longest suit, returning his suit will eventually set up at least one trick for the defense. He might have six spades, then declarer's queen will drop under the ace and North will have four winners to cash after South wins the ♦A.

In general, you should return partner's suit unless you have a very good reason not to. Here, a spade return also removes an entry for dummy's diamonds. So South plays the ♠4, ♠8, ♠6, ♠A.

In general return partner's suit

*Declarer plays the king of diamonds off the
dummy. What should South play?*

The one card South should not play is the ♦A.
If declarer has the ♦J, South cannot stop him
establishing the diamond suit but providing that
West has no more than three diamonds he can be
stopped from enjoying the suit later. East's entry, the
ace of spades, has already been knocked out so
South must duck the first two rounds of diamonds,
that is refuse to take the ace until the third round.

So, South plays the ♦3, declarer the ♦6 and
North the ♦5. Sure enough, the ♦2 is led off
dummy next and South keeps up the good work by
playing the ♦10, declarer winning the trick with the
♦J while North plays the ♦7. Now declarer leads a
low club, North takes the queen and continues with
the ♠7 which declarer wins with the queen. He
cashes two clubs, followed by two hearts but then
concedes the rest for one down. The full deal:

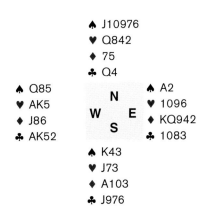

♠ J10976
♥ Q842
♦ 75
♣ Q4

♠ Q85	**N**	♠ A2
♥ AK5		♥ 1096
♦ J86	**W** **E**	♦ KQ942
♣ AK52	**S**	♣ 1083

♠ K43
♥ J73
♦ A103
♣ J976

Notice after the opening lead, declarer could see two tricks in spades, two tricks in hearts and two tricks in clubs so he needed three more. Obviously his best chance of getting these was to establish the diamond suit. He tried very hard to make South go wrong by leading the king off the dummy, but South resisted the temptation to win either of the first two tricks in diamonds, so West could only make two tricks in the suit. With eight tricks in the bag, West's best remaining chance was to try and make an extra trick from clubs. He would have succeeded if the defense's clubs had been divided 3-3 or if either defender had had ♣QJ doubleton, but when that failed to occur he needed an even greater miracle in the heart suit. As you can see, it didn't happen, so declarer finished one down.

Undoubtedly, East/West were unlucky. They were in the correct contract which was only beaten because:

(a) North chose to lead a spade.
(b) South had the ♠K rather than North.
(c) South returned a spade.
(d) The ♦A didn't appear on either of the first two rounds.
(e) The clubs didn't behave well for declarer.
(f) Neither defender was dealt ♥QJ doubleton.

North/South defended accurately and collected a bonus of just 50 points scored above the line.

points to remember

Don't be tempted to bid when the opponents are bidding strongly and you have garbage.

Defending against no trumps, it is normal to lead your longest suit; the idea being that it is the most likely source of tricks for the defense. Equally, it is normal to return partner's suit unless you have an obvious better alternative.

The lead of a minor honour such as the jack or queen tends to be the top of a sequence. So the queen promises at least the jack, and the jack promises at least the ten. You would also lead the jack from an interior sequence such as KJ109. When you hold the ace in dummy's long suit playing in no trumps, always consider not playing it before you have to, as frequently this can give declarer a problem with his communications.

Don't be tempted to bid when the opponents are bidding strongly and you have garbage.

deal 7

Dealer North
Neither side vulnerable. North/South +40

♠ 8643
♥ Q63
♦ QJ5
♣ AJ6

♠ 972
♥ A9742
♦ 1093
♣ 53

Would you open with North's hand?

No, he has an average hand with exactly 10 high card points and with no additional distributional points North should pass.

East opens 1NT. Of course, with only four points South passes. West raises to 3NT and everybody passes, so the complete bidding is:

South	West	North	East
–	–	Pass	1NT
Pass	3NT	Pass	Pass
Pass			

the play

What should South lead to give the best possible chance of beating 3NT?

Yes, of course, the ♥4, fourth best of South's longest and strongest suit. The West hand comes down as dummy revealing:

♠ KJ5
♥ J8
♦ K876
♣ KQ104

Declarer plays the ♥8 from the dummy, North plays the ♥Q and declarer plays the ♥K. At Trick 2, declarer leads the ♣9, South plays the ♣3, dummy contributes the ♣K and North wins the ♣A. At Trick 3, North leads the ♥6 and declarer plays the ♥5.

What card should South play now?

Of course, it is tempting to win the ♥A but, if South does, the defense can no longer beat the contract. South will only make one heart trick rather than three.

South knows that declarer has the ♥10, otherwise North would have played it at Trick 1, instead of the ♥Q, so South must hope that North has the ♥3 left. By letting declarer win the second round of hearts, South retains the ♥A as an entry for two more tricks if his partner gets the lead.

Here is the full deal:

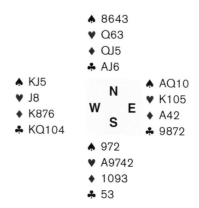

```
                          ♠ 8643
                          ♥ Q63
                          ♦ QJ5
                          ♣ AJ6
        ♠ KJ5                             ♠ AQ10
        ♥ J8            N                 ♥ K105
        ♦ K876      W       E             ♦ A42
        ♣ KQ104         S                 ♣ 9872
                          ♠ 972
                          ♥ A9742
                          ♦ 1093
                          ♣ 53
```

Notice that if declarer had four hearts and North two, South might not make the ace of hearts at all. However, all this would do is give East/West an extra 30 bonus points.

points to remember

Always concentrate on beating their contract

Defending against no trumps, unless partner has bid a suit, it is normal for you to lead fourth best of your longest and strongest suit. Always concentrate on beating the opponents' contract, do not worry about giving away overtricks. The duck can be a very effective way of maintaining communications for the defense.

deal 8

Dealer East
Neither side vulnerable. North/South +40

        ♠ K87
        ♥ 852
        ♦ A8
        ♣ J9765

        ♠ AQJ95
        ♥ K6
        ♦ 9752
        ♣ 104

This time East deals and opens one heart. What should South bid?

The South hand only has 10 high card points and even adding one distributional point for the five-card suit only brings the total to 11 – not enough to open the bidding. However, South should bid 1 ♠.

   The difference is that South is overcalling not opening the bidding. The criterion for overcalling is much more to do with playing strength than general strength measured in the form of points. A hand with just four straight aces would amount to 16 HCP, enough to open a strong no trump, but it would still only take four tricks. Given reasonable breaks and the expected heart lead, you would expect to make five tricks playing with spades as trumps with this South hand.

If we measure the strength in terms of points, then to overcall at the one level you require a good suit and a minimum of, say, eight points. For example, with just ♠AKJ107, it would be clear to overcall 1♠.

Like an opening bid, an overcall is generally aimed at finding your best available contract but getting into the bidding when the opponents have opened has a number of additional benefits. In particular, the overcall makes it harder for the opponents to bid their cards and, if they do end up playing the hand, your partner should know which suit to lead.

After South overcalls 1♠, West raises his partner's opening to 2♥.

An overcall makes it harder for your opponents

What should North bid now?

If South is likely to be able to scramble five tricks on his own, the ♠K and the ♦A should produce at least two more tricks, so North should be comfortable bidding two spades.

East passes, what should South do next?

South should be happy that North has been able to support him but, with nothing more than the minimum for the overcall, South should pass. The complete auction is:

South	West	North	East
–	–	–	1 ♥
1 ♠	2 ♥	2 ♠	Pass
Pass	Pass		

the play

West leads the seven of hearts and the North hand comes down as dummy.

How many winners has declarer got?

South has five winners in spades, the ♦A and, after the opening lead, a certain heart trick, making a total of seven tricks, so he needs just one more.

Where can this come from?

Setting up the clubs looks a pretty tall order, especially if the defense switch to diamonds after the first round. So the best shot is to try and make an extra trick by ruffing a diamond in the dummy. Let's see how the play goes.

East wins the opening lead with the ♥A and returns the suit to the king. South plays a diamond to the ace and another diamond, East wins the king and plays a trump. This makes the contract even safer. Declarer lets the spade run round to dummy's ♠8, crosses back to hand with a trump and then ruffs a diamond with the king of trumps in the dummy. Making eight tricks in all.

The lower your point count, the more important it is to have a good suit for an overcall.

South should be quite content with making the contract for another 60 points below the line, combined with the 40 South already scored in 1NT, this makes a game.

The full deal:

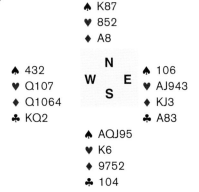

```
                    ♠ K87
                    ♥ 852
                    ♦ A8

    ♠ 432           N           ♠ 106
    ♥ Q107      W       E       ♥ AJ943
    ♦ Q1064         S           ♦ KJ3
    ♣ KQ2                       ♣ A83

                    ♠ AQJ95
                    ♥ K6
                    ♦ 9752
                    ♣ 104
```

points to remember

A one-level overcall does not promise opening bid values but it should promise a reasonable suit.

Partner should be happy to support your overcall at minimum level with three card support and a couple of useful looking cards.

Concentrate on reaching your target, do not endanger your contract by chasing after overtricks.

deal 9

Dealer South
North/South vulnerable

♠ 9875
♥ AKQ102
♦ KQ
♣ AQ

♠ K632
♥ 754
♦ 32
♣ KJ64

With only 7 HCP South passes. West also passes.

Now, what would you open with that North hand?

North has a very good heart suit and lots of points – a total of 20 points. However, North is not so strong that he needs to worry about missing a game if South can't drag up a response to a one-level opening. So, North should open 1 ♥.

East passes. What should South respond?

South should bid 1 ♠. South has more than five points so should bid in case North has in the region of 19 or 20. South should bid his four card spade suit, rather than 1NT, to make sure that North/South find an eight card spade fit if they have one.

West passes again. Now what should North rebid?

South's 1 ♠ bid showed at least four spades and at least six points. So, North knows that North/South have an eight card spade fit and at least 26 points, normally enough for game. North should raise to 4 ♠.

Both East and South pass but West comes to life choosing to double. There is nothing for either North or South to do but pass and take their medicine, so four spades doubled becomes the final contract.

The full auction is:

South	West	North	East
Pass	Pass	1 ♥	Pass
1 ♠	Pass	4 ♠	Pass
Pass	Dble	Pass	Pass
Pass			

the play

West leads the ♦ J and the North hand is dummy.

How many winners has declarer got?

Lots. At least three (and possibly five) in hearts, four in clubs, and one in diamonds after the ace has taken the first trick.

What about losers? Outside trumps, the only one is the ♦A, so, to make the contract, South needs to restrict his trump losers to two. Leading up to the king would succeed if the spades broke 3-2 and East had the ♠A.

Without any additional information, South would probably play this way but West's double suggests that it is unlikely that East has the ♠A and the trumps might not be breaking 3-2. Let's see. Declarer plays the the ♦Q from dummy and East duly takes his ace and returns the suit to West's nine and dummy's ♦K.

Now what should declarer do?

It would be annoying to lose too many trump tricks if the spades are 3-2 when, even if West has the ♠A, the contract would be at most one down just by playing trumps. On the other hand, if declarer play trumps now and East shows out, West will be able to draw trumps himself, conceding a trick to the ♠K and then ruff in with his fifth trump to cash three more diamond winners. South would certainly feel a bit sheepish having just become vulnerable and being well on the way to winning the rubber if he went five down in this contract conceding a penalty of 1400 points.

So declarer should start by cashing dummy's clubs and then start cashing dummy's hearts. The chances are that it will be West who will ruff which will shorten his trumps and leave you in control of the hand. Let's look at the full deal and see what happens:

Make sure that you keep trump control

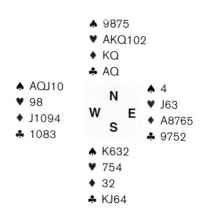

```
              ♠ 9875
              ♥ AKQ102
              ♦ KQ
              ♣ AQ
♠ AQJ10                      ♠ 4
♥ 98          N              ♥ J63
♦ J1094    W     E           ♦ A8765
♣ 1083        S              ♣ 9752
              ♠ K632
              ♥ 754
              ♦ 32
              ♣ KJ64
```

As you can see, fortunately, the trumps do not break 5-0, but the 4-1 break is quite bad enough.

If South tries to make the contract by playing a low spade to the king at Trick 3, the roof will fall in. West would draw all the remaining trumps and play on diamonds for five down and a 1400 penalty.

As it is, there is not much he can do. He can ruff the third round of hearts, but he can't play on trumps without giving up one of the five tricks the defence is entitled to.

Notice that, if South is brave enough to play a trump at an early stage then, as East actually has a trump, he can still make eight tricks provided that he doesn't sacrifice the king. Playing a low trump from both hands forces West to win with the ten and he still can't draw trumps as the king is protected. Still, two down doubled in a respectable game contract conceding a penalty of 500 points is not quite what South had in mind at the beginning of the deal.

points to remember

With six or more points you must respond if
partner opens with one of a suit as he might have
a strong enough hand for you to make
a game.

Remember that bridge is a game of
probabilities. If you are in what looks like a good
contract, which only fails because of a very poor
distribution of the cards, don't tell your partner off
for overbidding.

If you are doubled in your final contract, take
some care not to lose more tricks than you have
to. In particular, be suspicious that the
trumps are breaking badly.

The converse of this is that, if the
opponents bid game in a suit in
which you have a particularly
powerful holding, consider
making a penalty double.
A successful double
can increase your
score profitably.

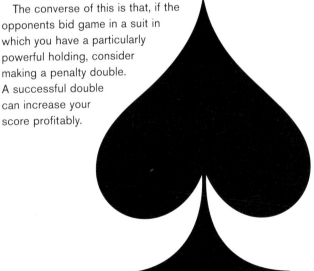

deal 10

Dealer West
North/South vulnerable

♠ A108
♥ 6
♦ 9654
♣ AKQ65

♠ KQJ97
♥ Q43
♦ A732
♣ 7

This time West deals and passes.

What should North open?

With 13 HCP (four in spades and nine in clubs) and one distributional point, North is strong enough to open the bidding. He should bid 1♣, his best suit.

East overcalls one heart. What should South bid?

With five good spades, South has an easy bid of 1♠. West competes, bidding 2♥.

What should North bid now?

Although North has only three spades, he has quite a good hand in support of spades especially as he only has one heart so, North should bid 2♠. It is particularly worth straining to support partner in a competitive auction because, if the bidding goes higher, partner can only judge what to do if he knows that, whenever you have reasonable support for his suit, you will support.

> **Support partner whenever you can**

East passes and it is South's turn once again. What should South bid now?

With an opening bid facing an opening bid, and knowledge of some spade support opposite, South should just bid 4♠. The complete auction is:

South	West	North	East
–	Pass	1♣	1♥
1♠	2♥	2♠	Pass
4♠	Pass	Pass	Pass

the play

West leads the ♠2 and the North hand is dummy.

How many tricks does South have?

Five spades, one diamond and three clubs makes a total of nine, so South needs one more.

Where can this come from?

The obvious route is to ruff a heart. The alternatives are ruffing a low club or establishing a diamond trick but both depend on even breaks in both the trump suit and the side suit. So declarer should win the ace of spades and play dummy's heart.

East rises with the ace and returns a second trump. South wins in hand, ruffs a heart with the ♠10, crosses back to the ♦A to draw trumps and cashes three clubs to make 10 tricks.

The full deal:

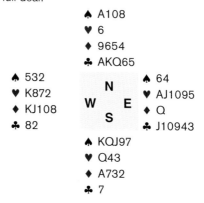

	♠ A108	
	♥ 6	
	♦ 9654	
	♣ AKQ65	
♠ 532		♠ 64
♥ K872	N	♥ AJ1095
♦ KJ108	W E	♦ Q
♣ 82	S	♣ J10943
	♠ KQJ97	
	♥ Q43	
	♦ A732	
	♣ 7	

The play would have been more difficult if East had returned a club as South would no longer have had an entry to dummy to cash the clubs later. However, without a trump return it is possible to ruff two hearts in the dummy, so South would only need two top clubs to make the contract. Notice that, if South tries to make an overtrick by cashing three clubs, West will ruff and return a trump leaving South one trick short of the ten trick target.

Making 4♠ scores 120 below the line and earns North/South a bonus of 700 points for winning the rubber two games to nil.

Here is the full scorecard:

	WE North/South	THEY East/West
(Rubber)	700	
(Deal 7)	50	
(Deal 6)	50	
(Deal 9)		500
(Deal 5)	40	
(Deal 8)	60	
(Deal 10)	120	
Totals	1020	500

North/South win the rubber by 520 points.

points to remember

It is more than acceptable to support partner with only three cards in competition.

When choosing your line of play, look for the alternative that is less dependent on the suits breaking. The more the opponents bid, the more likely the suits are to break badly.

deal 11

The ten remaining deals in this book are one-off deals. They are not organised into rubbers as you might get a false impression that it was your right always to hold good cards. However, on each deal you will be invited to consider the bidding from both South's and North's point of view, and then you will follow South in the play. Once again, it is difficult to work out your line of play just looking at the printed page in this text book, so get out a pack of cards and lay out both the North and South hands. At the end of the play, go over the deal again looking at all four hands.

```
              ♠ A4
              ♥ 86
              ♦ AK7532
              ♣ J76
                  N
              W       E
                  S
              ♠ J106
              ♥ AQ10
              ♦ 984
              ♣ AK42
```

What should North bid?

North has only 12 high card points but should add two distributional points for the fifth and sixth diamonds taking his total to 14. Plenty enough to open the bidding with 1♦.

East passes, now what should South do?

With 14 HCP facing an opening bid, South already knows that his side belong in game, but it is by no means clear which game. If South were to respond 2♣, and hear North rebid 2♦, what should South do next? He would still be none the wiser as to whether to play in 3NT or 5♦ but he would have little option but to guess which game to bid. Fortunately, there is an immediate response available to describe this sort of hand.

Two opening bids = game

What is it?

South should bid 2NT to show a balanced hand in the 13-15 HCP range. With such a good suit, North will rebid 3♦. Now South will still be concerned that his cover in spades is not very good, so he might bid 3♥ to test the waters. This covers North's weak spot, so North should be content to bid 3NT.

So the full bidding has been:

South	West	North	East
–	–	1♦	Pass
2NT	Pass	3♦	Pass
3♥	Pass	3NT	Pass
Pass	Pass		

the play

West leads the ♠K. Now plan the play.

How many top tricks does South have?

One spade, one heart, two diamonds and two clubs, a total of six, so South needs three more.

Where can these come from?

As a result of the lead, the spade suit is certain to provide another trick, and extra tricks might be made in both clubs and hearts, but the major source looks to be diamonds. If the opposing diamonds break 2-2, South can make four extra tricks. If diamonds breaks 3-1, South could establish three extra tricks by playing ace, king and another diamond.

What is the problem with this?

If he plays this way, South will establish the extra tricks but he will no longer have an entry back to dummy to cash the established diamonds.

What is the solution?

The answer is to duck an early round of diamonds. In this particular case, it is best to cash one top diamond just to make sure that the suit does not break 4-0 (in which case he would need to garner all his extra tricks from the outside suits) and, when both opponents follow, lead a low diamond at Trick 3. No matter who wins this trick, when South regains the lead he will be able to cross to dummy by playing his last diamond. The three additional diamonds ensure the contract.

It is true that, if the diamonds broke 2-2, South would make one less trick than he might have done. However, that is only an extra overtrick and by ducking the second round of diamonds he guaranteed making the contract whenever the suit broke 3-1.

The full deal:

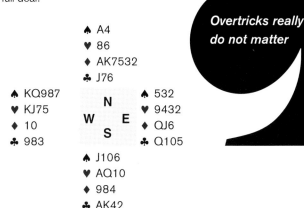

Overtricks really do not matter

```
                  ♠ A4
                  ♥ 86
                  ♦ AK7532
                  ♣ J76
    ♠ KQ987              ♠ 532
    ♥ KJ75       N       ♥ 9432
    ♦ 10      W     E    ♦ QJ6
    ♣ 983        S       ♣ Q105
                  ♠ J106
                  ♥ AQ10
                  ♦ 984
                  ♣ AK42
```

points to remember

The 2NT response to a one level suit opening is a good way of exploring for the best game.

Determine how many tricks you actually need from a suit before you decide how to play it.
East deals and opens 1 ♠.

deal 12

East deals and opens 1 ♠.

♠ 1065
♥ AQ10
♦ 984
♣ AQ105

```
      N
  W       E
      S
```

♠ A4
♥ 86
♦ AK7532
♣ J76

What would you bid as South after East opens 1 ♠?

With 12 HCP and a good six card diamond suit, South should overcall 2♦.

West passes. Now what should North do?

That is a much harder question inasmuch as North has a good enough hand to be in game, but with no ruffing power, 5♦ does not look that likely to make. North would prefer to play in 3NT provided that South has the spades covered. So, what can North do?

The answer is that North should bid the opponents' suit. Yes, North should bid 2♠. This shows a good hand and asks South to describe his hand further paying special attention as to whether he has a guard in spades or not. Over North's artificial 2♠ bid, South bids 2NT to show his spade stopper and North raises to 3NT. So the full bidding has been:

South	West	North	East
–	–	–	1♠
2♦	Pass	2♠	Pass
2NT	Pass	3NT	Pass
Pass	Pass		

the play

How many top tricks have you got?

West leads the ♠9. Plan the play?

First, how many top tricks has South got?

This time, South has one trick in spades, one in hearts, two in diamonds and one in clubs, a total of five, so South needs four more.

Where can extra tricks come from?

South might make an extra trick in hearts and South can make at least two more tricks in clubs. For example, if West had three clubs to the king, South could make three extra tricks by leading towards dummy's honours. The ten would win the first trick, and the queen the second., then the remaining clubs would fall under the ace. (This process of leading through opposing honours is known as finessing.) Finally, as on the last deal, South could make three or four extra tricks in diamonds.

Clearly, there are plenty of chances to generate extra tricks, so what is the problem with this hand?

The problem is that South knows that East started with at least five spades, so, as soon as the defense get the lead, they will be able to take four tricks in spades. So, South really cannot afford to duck a diamond. Worse still, as East opened the bidding he is likely to have both the ♥K and the ♣K, so taking a finesse in either suit is a recipe for disaster.

Remember to unblock the diamonds!

So, what should South do?

He really has no option but to play out the diamonds from the top and hope they are 2-2, in which case all four extra tricks will come from diamonds.

One further point, unless South is careful he could find that the diamonds break 2-2 and he still doesn't make his contract.

Why is that?

The problem is that, when he cashes the ♦A and ♦K, he must be very careful to play the ♦8 and the ♦9 from the dummy. Otherwise, he will 'block the suit', forced to win the third round of the suit in dummy and he will never be able to get back to his own hand.

Have a look at the full deal:

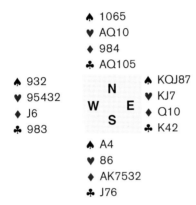

```
              ♠ 1065
              ♥ AQ10
              ♦ 984
              ♣ AQ105
♠ 932                        ♠ KQJ87
♥ 95432         N            ♥ KJ7
♦ J6         W     E         ♦ Q10
♣ 983           S            ♣ K42
              ♠ A4
              ♥ 86
              ♦ AK7532
              ♣ J76
```

points to remember

A bid in the opponents' suit is frequently used to ask partner to describe his hand further. It normally shows good values but no sensible alternative bid.

It is no good establishing the extra tricks you need if this means that your opponents can take enough tricks to beat you first. In these circumstances you should look for a line of play that gives you a chance of reaching your target first.

When trying to cash a long suit in one hand, be careful to 'unblock' high cards from the other hand.

deal 13

♠ 85
♥ AK2
♦ J1042
♣ 9653

```
      N
  W       E
      S
```

♠ A42
♥ Q54
♦ AKQ
♣ K742

Once more South has dealt himself a strong balanced hand.

How many points does South actually have?

Four in spades, two in hearts, nine in diamonds and three in clubs makes a total of 18.

So what should be South's choice of opening bid?

With 16-18 points and a balanced hand, open 1NT.

After West passes the spotlight turns on North. How many points does North have?

Seven points in hearts and one in diamonds makes a total of eight.

Now North knows quite a lot about the hand. His partner, South, has shown between 16 and 18 points so he knows that his side has between 24 and 26 points.

With two balanced hands you will normally need at least 25 points to make 3NT a sensible proposition. Now North is in an interesting position – if partner is minimum he cannot expect to take more than eight tricks but if South is maximum North/South could sensibly play in 3NT.

So what can North bid to find out whether South is minimum or maximum?

North can invite South to go on to game with a maximum by bidding 2NT. This suggests that North has enough to make 2NT if South is minimum and that 3NT should be possible if South has a maximum.

East passes and the spot-light falls back on South.

What should South bid now?

Partner invited South to bid game if maximum. As he has 18 points, the top of the possible range, South should bid on to 3NT.

There is no further bidding so the whole auction is:

South	West	North	East
1NT	Pass	2NT	Pass
3NT	Pass	Pass	Pass

the play

West leads the ♠6. Count your top tricks

Eight. The ace of spades, the ace, king, queen of hearts and four tricks in diamonds provided that South remembers to take the top diamonds in his hand before using both of dummy's heart entries. So, to make nine tricks, South needs one more.

Where can this come from?

If he leads a club from dummy towards the king then he can make an extra trick, if East has the ♣A. Let's try playing the hand. West has led the ♠6, North plays low and East will play the ♠K.

What should South play at Trick 1?

Here is the full deal:

```
              ♠ 85
              ♥ AK2
              ♦ J1042
              ♣ 9653

♠ Q10763          N          ♠ KJ9
♥ 983                        ♥ J1076
♦ 986         W       E      ♦ 753
♣ Q10             S          ♣ AJ8

              ♠ A42
              ♥ Q54
              ♦ AKQ
              ♣ K742
```

Look and see what happens if South wins the ♠A.

South starts by taking three top diamonds, then crosses to the ♥K to cash the last diamond. South discards a club while both opponents throw hearts. Then declarer plays a club towards the king.

The good news is that, as East has the ♣A, the king is established as the ninth trick.

The bad news is that, after taking the ace of clubs, East plays the ♠J which holds the trick and then another spade enabling West to take three more spade tricks to beat the contract.

Now, look at the hand again, and see what happens if South refuses to take the ♠A until the third round of spades. South plays the ♠2 on the first trick. East continues with the ♠J and South plays the ♠4. Then when East plays the ♠9, South takes the ♠A, discarding a club from the dummy.

Then, he cashes three top diamonds, crosses to a top heart to cash the last diamond and plays a club. As before, East rises with the ♣A but now he has no more spades to play. Yes, West has two more winners but he has no entry available to take them.

Notice that, if East had another spade to put West in with, then West could only have had a four card suit to start with.

This technique of refusing a trick that you could win is known as ducking. This is a useful weapon to sever communications between the defending hands.

By refusing to win either of the first two rounds of spades you were able to make nine tricks, and your contract, for a score of 100 points.

points to remember

The raise of 1NT to 2NT is a limit bid. Opener is invited to bid on to game with a maximum and pass with a minimum.

Notice the importance of leading up towards unsupported honours to make extra tricks. By and large, the king in a suit will make a trick if the opposing ace is on the right side provided you lead towards the king and not away from it.

In planning the play you need to consider not only how you can establish the right number of tricks for you to succeed in your contract but also how you can stop the opponents from cashing too many winners before you can take yours.

deal 14

♠ Q642
♥ 4
♦ AJ10942
♣ A3

♠ J75
♥ AK752
♦ K
♣ K1042

Would you open the bidding with the North hand?

Although North only has 11 high card points, he should open the bidding with this distributional hand. In point count terms he can add one point for for both the fifth and the sixth diamonds. The two extra points take the total point count to the magic target of 13, enough to open the bidding.

Obviously there is no guarantee that he will get to play in either diamonds or spades when North's ruffing strength will be important. However, even in no trumps the hand is worth much more than 11 points as you might make extra tricks with the long diamonds.

So, what should North open?

With a distributional hand, it is right to bid the longest suit first. So North should open 1♦.

East passes, and attention turns to the South hand. With 14 high card points facing an opening bid, South already knows that he has enough for game – but which one?

If partner has some heart support, 4♥ is the likely destination but it is quite possible that this hand should be played in 3NT, 5♣ or even 5♦, so South need more information to help choose the contract.

What should South bid now?

South should respond 1♥ asking partner to support hearts if he can or to make another bid to describe his hand. There is no need to jump to 2♥ as a change of suit forces North to bid again.

West passes, and again we look at the North hand. What rebid should North make now?

It does look tempting to rebid the diamond suit but it is right to bid 1♠ not 2♦. The rebid of 1♠ shows a distributional hand with both diamonds and spades – and, as we always bid our longer suit first, South should expect longer diamonds than spades.

East passes again. What should South bid now?

Now, South has already shown his hearts and North has bid both diamonds and spades. South has the strength to bid game, no good fit in either of partner's suits and a fairly good holding in clubs. A jump to 3NT seems to say it all.

So, the whole auction has been:

South	West	North	East
–	Pass	1 ♦	Pass
1 ♥	Pass	1 ♠	Pass
3NT	Pass	Pass	Pass

the play

West leads the ♣6, the North hand appears as dummy and once again South must try to make nine tricks in no trumps. Step 1. Count the top tricks.

South has six top tricks, two in hearts, two in diamonds and two in clubs. So declarer needs three more.

Where can they come from?

With a lot of luck, South might make two extra tricks in spades and one in hearts but we would have to lose two tricks in both suits to achieve this, by which time the defenders would have established their clubs. So, the only sensible way to try and make three extra tricks is to play on diamonds.

What card should declarer play from dummy on the opening lead?

Declarer must play ♣3 as he will need the ♣A as an entry later, so win the first trick in the South hand. At Trick 2, South leads the ♦K, West plays the ♦3.

What card do you play from the dummy?

If South plays a low diamond from the dummy and then crosses to the ♣A to cash the ♦A , he will only make three extra tricks when either opponent has a singleton or a doubleton ♦Q, and then declarer will make four extra tricks and not three. Declarer should recognise that, overall, he only needs five tricks in diamonds to make the contract (not six) and that means that South can afford to lose one diamond trick provided that this establishes the suit while he still has the ♣A as an entry to the dummy. So, declarer should overtake the ♦K with the ace, and then lead the ♦J to knock out the queen. In this way, he will make five diamond tricks whenever the diamonds are divided 3-3 or 4-2, no matter where the ♦Q is, and he will also succeed if either defender has a singleton ♦Q. It doesn't matter what the opponents do, for after taking the ♦Q they only have two top tricks to cash and South can get to the dummy with the ♣A for all those diamond winners.

It is worth noting that the ♦Q will be doubleton about 16% of the time, whereas the diamonds will break 3-3 or 4-2 about 84% of the time. So overtaking the ♦ K with the ♦ A is much the better play, succeeding more than five times as often.

The full deal:

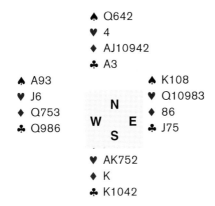

```
              ♠ Q642
              ♥ 4
              ♦ AJ10942
              ♣ A3
♠ A93                        ♠ K108
♥ J6              N          ♥ Q10983
♦ Q753        W     E        ♦ 86
♣ Q986           S           ♣ J75
              ♥ AK752
              ♦ K
              ♣ K1042
```

points to remember

If you bid two suits of your own, partner will expect you to have a distributional not a balanced hand. Sometimes, of course, both suits will have the same length but, in general, partner should expect you to have more cards in your first bid suit than your second. Here, five diamonds and four spades.

If you are trying to make extra tricks in one particular suit, consider how many tricks you need from that suit in total. This should tell you how many tricks you can afford to lose in the suit in order to establish the necessary number of winners.

deal 15

Dealer East who opens 1 ♥.

♠ AJ109
♥ A65
♦ K42
♣ 753

```
        N
   W        E
        S
```

♠ KQ83
♥ 4
♦ AQ65
♣ Q862

South has enough points to open the bidding so it is rather frustrating for him to hear East open 1 ♥ as he has no long suit to bid.

What can South do?

In the good old days there was nothing that South could really do other than overcall 1 ♠ on a four card suit but this is a fairly dangerous procedure especially as partner would expect at least five cards in the suit. However, then it was decided that as the chance of holding a hand where you wanted to double on the first round to say that the opponents couldn't make their contract was very low, a first round double of a suit opening could sensibly be used conventionally rather than as a penalty double. So the takeout double was born.

The idea is that if you double a suit opening on the first round you are showing opening bid values with support for the three unbid suits. Ideally, this should show a shortage in the opponents suit, so the South hand looks to be perfect for this action. Accordingly, South should double.

West passes, now what should North bid?

From North's points of view, if South is short in hearts and doesn't have a decent 5-card suit then there must be a good chance of South holding four spades. In that case, 4♠ looks to be a sensible contract. Indeed, if North had to choose the contract in one go, he should bid 4♠.

However, as there is a chance that South has a stronger hand without four spades, North chooses to bide his time and bid 2♥.

Once again, the bid in the opponent's suit shows a good hand and asks partner to describe his hand.

So, in this case, South would bid 2♠ to confirm that he has four cards in the suit and North would raise to 4♠.

The full bidding is:

South	West	North	East
–	–	–	1♥
Dble	Pass	2♥	Pass
2♠	Pass	4♠	Pass
Pass	Pass		

the play

West leads the ten of hearts. How many tricks has South got?

Off the top there are four spade tricks, one heart trick and three diamond tricks. A total of eight, so South needs two more.
One trick could come from the fourth diamond, if the diamonds break 3-3.
Another trick could come from clubs if East who did open the bidding has both the ace and king or South could make extra tricks by ruffing. For example, if trumps break 3-2, declarer could draw trumps and cash the diamonds. If the diamonds break 3-3 South will be able to throw a club from the dummy and eventually ruff a club for the tenth trick. If the diamonds don't break then he can ruff the fourth diamond in dummy and hope to make an extra trick out of clubs.

That is not a totally silly plan, but can South do any better?

Yes, why not plan to ruff two hearts in the South hand and then draw trumps with dummy's spades?

So, win with dummy's ♥A and ruff a heart immediately with the ♠Q, then cross back to dummy with a trump and play dummy's last heart ruffing with the ♠K. Then, South can play his last trump and draw all the opposing trumps before touching the diamonds at all.

In effect South will have made six trump tricks, the ♥A and the ♦AKQ – 10 tricks in all and if the diamonds break 3-3 he will make an overtrick. This play is not dependent on anything good happening in either minor suit and it will even succeed if either defender has four trumps.

The full deal:

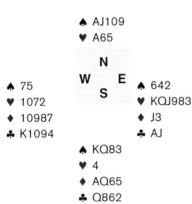

♠ AJ109
♥ A65

♠ 75   ♠ 642
♥ 1072   ♥ KQJ983
♦ 10987   ♦ J3
♣ K1094 ♣ AJ

♠ KQ83
♥ 4
♦ AQ65
♣ Q862

points to remember

If you have opening bid values with no long suit to overcall and support for the three suits not bid by your opponent, then you can make a takeout double.

In looking to make extra tricks by ruffing, sometimes it will be possible to ruff in your own hand and draw trumps in dummy. This is known as a dummy reversal.

deal 16

Dealer West who opens 1 ♥.

♠ A4
♥ AK7
♦ Q753
♣ KQ63

```
      N
  W       E
      S
```

♠ 986532
♥ 32
♦ 106
♣ 742

After West's opening, what should North bid?

North has 18 HCP and with a good heart holding
North should bid 1NT. This means the same as if
North had opened the bidding to start with.

East passes, now what should South do?

With no high card points at all, South
might be tempted to pass, but in
1NT the South hand will take no
tricks at all whereas, playing in
spades, the South hand might be
worth about three tricks. So South
should bid 2 ♠.

Everybody passes so the full bidding
has been:

South	West	North	East
–	1♥	1NT	Pass
2♠	Pass	Pass	Pass

the play:

*West leads the queen of hearts. How many top
tricks does South have?*

South has one trick in spades and two in hearts,
so he needs five more.

Where can these come from?

If trumps break 3-2, South will make three long
trump tricks and the club suit might provide two
more if West holds the ♣A, provided clubs are led
from the South hand.
   So, declarer wins the ♥A and plays the ♠A and
another trump. If trumps break 4-1 there is nothing to
do but declarer would not like to lose extra trump
tricks by letting the defence ruff when the trumps
break 3-2. West wins the ♠Q and plays the ♥J.

South wins with the king and plays what next?

It doesn't matter what South plays provided it is
not a club. The plan is to ruff a heart in South to
play a club to the queen. When this holds, South

will play a diamond off the dummy. The defence can take another spade and two diamonds but eventually they must either play a club themselves or let South in to play another club towards the king.

Now, you can see the power of playing in a long suit. Playing in 1NT , North would have made just four tricks but playing in spades South made eight. Here is the full deal:

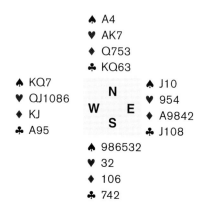

♠ A4
♥ AK7
♦ Q753
♣ KQ63

♠ KQ7
♥ QJ1086
♦ KJ
♣ A95

N
W E
S

♠ J10
♥ 954
♦ A9842
♣ J108

♠ 986532
♥ 32
♦ 106
♣ 742

points to remember

If partner has opened or overcalled 1NT and you have a weak hand with a 5 card or longer suit, consider playing in your long suit. With the exception of 2♣ and a bid of the opponents' suit, two level bids are weak take-outs.

Never waste your entries to the weak hand, use them to lead up towards the high cards opposite.

deal 17

♠ QJ109
♥ AK42
♦ 652
♣ 82

        N
    W   E
        S

♠ AK85
♥ 53
♦ AK7
♣ Q753

What do you open with the South hand?

South has seven points in both spades and
diamonds and two in clubs making a total of 16.
As the hand is balanced and in the required
range, South should open 1NT yet again.

*West passes, what should
North do?*

With 10 points facing a 1NT
opening, North should already know
that his side has enough for game,
so he could just bid 3NT. However, on
most deals it is better to play in a major
suit game rather than 3NT if there are at
least eight trumps between the two hands.

There are two main reasons for this:

(a) Playing in a suit contract stops the opponents from making too many tricks in their best suit as declarer will be able to ruff eventually.

(b) Playing with a trump suit offers many extra ways of making tricks by ruffing.

So, in practice North would like to play this deal in 3NT if South has no 4-card major, in 4♥ if South has four hearts or in 4♠ if South has four spades.

Stayman helps you to find a 4-4 fit in a major suit.

How can we find this out?

The easiest way is by adopting the Stayman convention. This is a totally artificial bid used all over the world in response to 1NT. A response of 2♣ after partner has opened 1NT asks opener to bid:

(a) 2♦ with no four card major.
(b) 2♥ with four hearts.
(c) 2♠ with four spades without four hearts.

So, with this hand, North should bid 2♣.

East passes, so what should South bid now?

North has asked a question. Has South got a four card major? Yes, obviously, South has four spades and not four hearts so South should bid 2♠.

West passes again and so it is North's turn. What should North bid now?

North now knows that his partnership has an eight-card fit in spades. A raise to just 3♠ would be invitational, asking South to bid on with a maximum, but North already knows that they have enough points to play in game, so North should bid 4♠.

East passes again, and once more South is in the hot seat. What should South do now? South has described his hand pretty accurately and North has selected the final contract of 4♠, so you should pass.

West passes once again, so the full auction is:

South	West	North	East
1NT	Pass	2♣	Pass
2♠	Pass	4♠	Pass
Pass	Pass		

the play

West leads the ♠2, the North hand comes down as dummy, and South has to try and make 10 tricks with spades as trumps.

How many top winners does South have?

South has four spade tricks, two hearts and two diamonds, making a total of eight. So South needs two more tricks to make the contract. There is no long suit to set up so the extra tricks must come from ruffing.

Should South try ruffing hearts in his own hand or clubs in the dummy?

To ruff the clubs in dummy South would have to lose the lead in clubs twice. This would allow the defense to play two more rounds of trumps – thereby restricting declarer to just one club ruff. So, South must try to ruff hearts. The plan is to ruff both of dummy's small hearts in the South hand. Suppose declarer wins the opening lead with the ♠9 in dummy. Then he should cash the ♦A and ♦K (to guard against them being ruffed later) and play the ♥A, ♥K and another heart ruffing in the South hand.

What card should South ruff with?

South must ruff the heart with either the ♠A or the ♠K. Ruffing high retains the ♠8 to cross to dummy with in order to ruff the last remaining heart with a high trump.

At this stage South will have taken eight tricks: the opening trump, two diamonds, two top hearts, a heart ruff high, a trump back to the dummy and another heart ruff and South will still have two good trumps sitting in the dummy to make up his ten tricks.

The full deal:

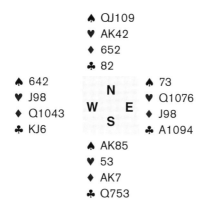

```
                ♠ QJ109
                ♥ AK42
                ♦ 652
                ♣ 82
♠ 642                        ♠ 73
♥ J98        N               ♥ Q1076
♦ Q1043   W     E            ♦ J98
♣ KJ6        S               ♣ A1094
                ♠ AK85
                ♥ 53
                ♦ AK7
                ♣ Q753
```

points to remember

On most deals it is better to play in a major suit rather than no trumps if you have at least eight trumps between you.

The Stayman convention is designed to help you find a 4-4 major fit after a 1NT opening. A bid of 2♣ asks opener to bid a four card major if he has one, otherwise he should bid 2♦.

Be careful to make sure that you have enough entries to take however many ruffs you need before you start ruffing.

deal 18

♠ 93
♥ KJ92
♦ Q64
♣ AK42

```
      N
W         E
      S
```

♠ KQ752
♥ AQ74
♦ 53
♣ J6

This time North deals himself a balanced hand with 13 high card points.

What should North bid?

With a balanced hand and 13 HCP, North should open the bidding but, as he is not strong enough to open 1NT, North must open with a suit bid. He should not bid 1♥ as this would show at least five hearts, so North really has no choice but to open 1♣.

In fact, this bid does not even guarantee that North holds a club suit. With a 4-3-3-3 distribution and a four card major you have to open 1♣. Similarly, if your distribution is 4-4-2-3 going down the suits, you also open 1♣ but with 4-4-3-2 including three diamonds and two clubs, you open 1♦.

East passes and you have to decide what to do with the South hand?

With an opening bid of his own, South should expect to reach game when North opens, however on this deal it could be right to play in 3NT, 4♥ or 4♠ or even 5♣. How can South find out?

   South should start by bidding his longest suit. So, South responds 1♠.

West passes. Then what rebid should North make?

North should rebid 1NT. This shows a balanced hand of 13-15 HCP; in other words, a hand that was not strong enough to open 1NT.

East passes again. What should South bid next?

South should bid 3♥. The jump to 3♥ is forcing (meaning that North must bid again) and shows at least five spades and at least four hearts. North is invited to support hearts with four, show delayed support for spades with three cards or rebid 3NT.

West passes, and once again, North is in the hot seat. What should North bid now?

North knows that South has at least five spades and four hearts and that he is exploring for an eight card fit. With four hearts, as on this hand, North must support by bidding 4♥.

East passes, so, what should South do?

South should pass. With only 12 points facing a maximum of 15, it would be far too optimistic to look for a slam. So, the full auction has been:

West	North	East	South
–	1♣	Pass	1♠
Pass	1NT	Pass	3♥
Pass	4♥	Pass	Pass
Pass			

the play

West leads the ♣10, the North hand goes down as dummy and South has to make 10 tricks with hearts as trumps.

How many top tricks are there?

Let's play along these lines and see what happens.

There are six obvious top tricks, four in hearts and two in clubs. So, that means that declarer needs to find four extra tricks. He could get one by ruffing a diamond in South, and perhaps another one if he ruffed a club as well. However, to get another four tricks, South must tackle the spade suit.

If both defenders have three spades this should not be too difficult. South could lead up to the spade honours twice and if East has the ace of spades the suit will be established

without having to ruff. However, if West has the
♠A, declarer will need to ruff a spade to establish
two small spades winners in the South hand.
Let's play along these lines and see what happens.

*First, what card should South play from
dummy at trick one?*

South could play a low club hoping that
West has led away from the queen, but if
East has the queen this will spell instant
defeat losing one club, two diamonds and
a spade and, even if successful, it would only
generate one extra trick rather than four. So
South should win the first trick with one of the
top clubs in dummy, say the king.

*What should declarer play from dummy at t
rick two?*

There is no point in trying to draw trumps until the
spade suit is established, so declarer should lead
a spade off the dummy immediately.

East plays low and the queen holds the trick.

Now South can cash the ace of hearts and play
the ♥4 to the king, noting the fact that both
opponents follow so there is only one trump out.
Now he leads a second spade – and East takes
the ace. East leads the ♦2. West wins the ♦A
and returns the ♦J covered by dummy's ♦Q and
East's king. Then, East plays a third diamond.

What card do should South play?

Yes, of course, South must ruff this with the ♥ 7.
   Now, what card should declarer lead from the South hand for the next trick?
Let's look at the remaining cards:

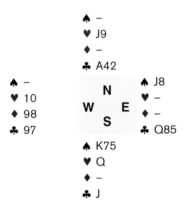

```
              ♠ –
              ♥ J9
              ♦ –
              ♣ A42
   ♠ –                    ♠ J8
   ♥ 10        N          ♥ –
   ♦ 98     W     E       ♦ –
   ♣ 97        S          ♣ Q85
              ♠ K75
              ♥ Q
              ♦ –
              ♣ J
```

As you can see, spades were not actually divided 3-3. Had they been, declarer would be able to succeed by drawing the outstanding trump with the ♥Q and then cashing the spades from the top. However, as it is, East would still have a master spade, so that plan will not work.

   It is essential to lead a small spade now and ruff it in the dummy, declarer can even afford to ruff with the ♥J. Then cross back to the South hand with the last trump, drawing West's last trump *en route*, and the two remaining spades and dummy's ace of clubs will take the last three tricks.

The full deal:

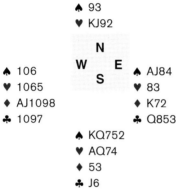

```
              ♠ 93
              ♥ KJ92
                    N
  ♠ 106       W       E      ♠ AJ84
  ♥ 1065           S         ♥ 83
  ♦ AJ1098                   ♦ K72
  ♣ 1097                     ♣ Q853
              ♠ KQ752
              ♥ AQ74
              ♦ 53
              ♣ J6
```

points to remember

Opening the bidding with one of a suit and rebidding 1NT shows a balanced hand with 13-15 points.

After a 1NT rebid by opener, a jump in a new suit by responder forces opener to bid again (unless responder jumps to game).

If you are trying to establish a side suit, it is important to try and lead towards your honour combinations and not away from them.

If you need to ruff a side suit to establish it remember that you are going to need an entry back to that hand after the suit is established.

deal 19

♠ 532
♥ K54
♦ KQ108
♣ KQ6

```
        N
    W       E
        S
```

♠ QJ10864
♥ A9
♦ J97
♣ A5

As dealer, what should South bid?

Although South has only 12 high card points, to open one of a suit he can count distributional points as well. One point for any card more than four in any suit. So, the six card spade suit is worth two additional points taking the total to 14. South bids 1 ♠.

West passes, so now let's consider the North hand. How many points does North have?

North has three points in hearts, five in diamonds and five in clubs making 13 in all.

With an opening bid facing an opening bid, you should play in game – however, so far, North has no idea which will be the best game. It seems likely to be 3NT but if the opener has a distributional hand it could easily be 4♠ or even 5♦.

It is convenient that we have a response to an opening suit bid to show game-going values and a balanced hand leaving room to explore further.

What is it?

If you haven't passed already, a response of 2NT shows a balanced hand of 13-15 points.

East passes, now what should South do?

Partner has shown a balanced hand with game-going values so with an extra card in spades (remember 1♠ promised a 5-card suit) and good intermediates South should know that 4♠ must be a reasonable contract. Accordingly, South should just bid 4♠.

West passes, and the action goes back to North. What should North do now?

North has given a good description of his hand and South has chosen the contract based on that . North should pass and let South get on with it.

So, the bidding has been:

If you have described your hand well, let partner take the decision

South	West	North	East
1♠	Pass	2NT	Pass
4♠	Pass	Pass	Pass

the play

West leads the ♦A and when everyone follows he continues with the ♦2.

After the opening lead there are plenty of tricks, two top hearts, three in diamonds, three in clubs and four in spades after knocking out the ace and king.

So, how many top losers does declarer have?

There are three top losers, the ♦A and the ♠AK.

Is there any danger of losing another trick?

Yes. If West has a doubleton diamond and East wins the first spade trick, West might score a diamond ruff. If West started with three trumps, this will beat the contract unless something is done.

Can you see any way of stopping West from making a cheap trump trick?

Win the diamond and then play the ace, king and queen of clubs discarding South's third diamond. Then play a small spade from the dummy.

East wins the spade ace and plays another diamond. Which card should South play now?

Not only must South ruff, he must ruff with one of his top spades otherwise West will make a trick with the ♠9. South can then play a top trump.

West will win but whatever West returns South will
be able to win and draw the last trump.

The full deal:

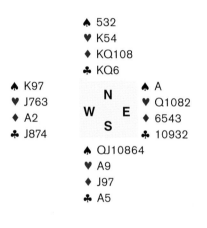

```
                    ♠ 532
                    ♥ K54
                    ♦ KQ108
                    ♣ KQ6
      ♠ K97              N        ♠ A
      ♥ J763                      ♥ Q1082
      ♦ A2          W        E    ♦ 6543
      ♣ J874            S         ♣ 10932
                    ♠ QJ10864
                    ♥ A9
                    ♦ J97
                    ♣ A5
```

points to remember

The immediate response of 2NT to a
one level suit opener shows a
balanced hand and about 13-15
points. In effect, the bid
announces that you have the
values to make game but leaves
space for you to explore all the
possible options.

Playing in a suit contract, if you find that you
have plenty of winners then it is
right to count your losers.

deal 20

♠ AQ5
♥ 654
♦ KQJ6
♣ 542

```
      N
  W       E
      S
```

♠ K62
♥ AKQ10
♦ A53
♣ AJ10

South has dealt himself another very strong hand. South has three points in spades, nine in hearts, four in diamonds and five in clubs; a total of 21 points.

What is South's opening bid?

With a balanced hand of 21 or 22 points South should open 2NT. Note that with a hand of 19 or 20 points South would be too strong to open 1NT but not strong enough to open 2NT. With that type of hand he would open with a one-level suit bid, planning to jump in no trumps to show his strength.

West passes and it is North's turn. The strength of South's hand limits the other three players to sharing out 18 or 19 between them so North should be pleased to have been dealt 12 of them.

So, what is North/South's combined point count?

21 or 22 in the South hand plus 12 in North yields a total of 33 or 34 points. With 33 points between the two hands, North should know that his side cannot be missing two aces so there should be a reasonable chance of making 12 tricks.

> ### 33 points is enough for a small slam

So, what should North bid?

With no ruffing values in the North hand, it is not worth looking for a suit fit. Very simply, North should bid what he thinks his side can make – 6NT.
    East passes again giving South another turn.

What should South bid now?

South should pass. He has defined his hand within a narrow range and North, his partner, has chosen 6NT as the contract. South should respect that decision and pass.

So, the bidding is:

South	West	North	East
2NT	Pass	6NT	Pass
Pass	Pass		

the play

West leads the ♦10 Plan the play.

How many top tricks does declarer have?

There are 11 top tricks: three in spades, three in hearts, four in diamonds and one in clubs. To make 6NT, you need 12 tricks, so South only needs to find one more which might come from hearts or clubs. Just looking at the heart suit alone, start by cashing the ace and king. If West shows out on the second round, cross to the dummy and play a heart to the 10. Alternatively, if the jack appears on the second round then the 10 is good.

If nothing nice happens on the second round, should South:

(a) Play low from dummy towards the Q10 intending to play the 10 if East follows low, or

(b) Cash the queen hoping that the jack will fall?

If South plays a low heart from dummy and East follows with a low card, the problem reduces to who is more likely to hold the last heart. West is more likely to have the last heart as he has one more card left than East at this point. So, South should play the queen hoping to drop the jack. In other words, line (b) is a little better than line (a). Overall, cashing the three top hearts will produce an extra trick getting on for 60% of the time.

What about the club suit? Playing them out from the top South would need to be exceptionally lucky to make more than one trick, however, consider what happens if he leads up to the AJ10 twice.

On the first occasion, East plays low so South puts in the ten which loses to West's king. Then South goes back to dummy to lead a second club towards the remaining AJ. If East has the queen, and plays low, South can take the trick with the jack.

This play in clubs, known as a double finesse, will produce an extra trick whenever East has either or both of the missing club honours. It will succeed just over 75% of the time. It will only fail if West has both the king and the queen.

So, if South just had to play on one suit, it would be much better to play on clubs than hearts, but he can do much better still by playing on both suits. Let's look and see how the whole play should go.

South takes the opening diamond lead with the jack to play a club to the ten and king. He wins the diamond continuation with the ace and cashes two top hearts, if West shows out, he can safely cross to dummy and play a heart to the ten.

Assuming both opponents follow to the two hearts, cash a third heart, if the jack appears, he has 12 tricks.

Assuming nothing nice happens, he cashes three spade tricks and two diamond tricks discarding the ♥10 on the last diamond unless the ♥J has already appeared. Finally, at trick 12, if all else has failed, he plays a club from the dummy intending to play the jack unless East plays the queen.

The full deal:

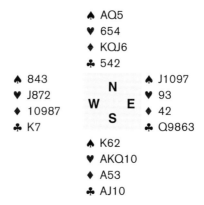

points to remember

An opening bid of 2NT shows a balanced hand with about 21-22 points.

If you know that your side has at least 33 points, you should be looking to play in at least a small slam.

A suit in which you can take a double finesse gives you better than a 75% chance of making an extra trick provided that you lead up to your honours.

Look for ways of increasing your chances of making a contract by combining plays in more than one suit.